Hollie McNish

Papers

GREENWICH EXCHANGE

LONDON

Greenwich Exchange, London

First published in Great Britain in 2012
All rights reserved

Papers © Hollie McNish 2012

Printed and bound by imprintdigital.net
Cover image and design: Inua Ellams

Greenwich Exchange Website: www.greenex.co.uk

Cataloguing in Publication Data is available
from the British Library

ISBN: 978-1-906075-67-5

Hollie McNish

Papers

DILEMMA

19/04/10 Dilemma 23.32pm Age 27

When she finally sleeps, I mean *finally* sleeps
like that eyes roll back, lips apart deep kinda sleep
no peeks eyes relaxed, close, naks this kinda sleep
heavy breath sleep to mean the beauty in sleep.
When she finally sleeps, I mean *finally* sleeps
and our bed sheets haven't been seen for days kinda sleep
and it seems we've got three full hours before her next feed
and we sneak into bed and our legs want to weep,
finally, lying down, her father and me
the dilemma appears like a newborn brutally *brutality*
'cause she finally sleeps, we can finally be
skin to skin, cuddled under the covers in gl
our giggling eyelids smile heavily
as we shoosh at each sound that might wake
One kiss on your cheek to tell you goodnight
one kiss on your lips and a hand to your thighs
as your head wants to dream and there isn't much
but the warmth of the back of your body on mine
three hours turns to two to tease me awake
and your breath feels so good on my aching neck
but each kiss that I give is one more minute awake
and I haven't slept well for at least seven days,
if I carry the play on, keep touching your face
we won't get the sleep our minds desperately crave,
fulfilling a space my skin endings ache

To Mum. Dad. Al. Gee. Z. Papa. Grandpa. Gaga and Gran x
I'm sure you won't like a lot of these,
I hope you find at least a couple in here that you do!

CONTENTS

PAPER

She is safe.
To walk the streets and fields and forests alone.
Wearing no clothes.
But cloaked in sheets of paper printed with the
'UN Universal Declaration of Human Rights'.
Paper shoes, paper pants, paper jumper, paper hat,
the words wrap around her body.
A paper blanket proclaiming her 'legal human rights'.
'The Right not to be Hungry'.
Her stomach rumbles,
So she rips a piece of paper from her paper shirt and swallowing the scrumpled words paper
cuts cover her gums and her stomach rumbles again,
treading slowly in paper shoes through farm fields bare of seed or rain, she bends and buries
small cuttings of paper grain and watches as their paper leaves spout from the dry earth
        declaring her
'Right not to be Hungry'.
But she is safe.
She has the Universal Human Right not to be Raped.
So she walks to work at night
and frightened as he grabs her paper sleeve and slaps her face, rips her paper pants apart and
disgraces her, she slumps against the wall, pulls up her paper skirt and matches up the words,
ripped pieces of her paper pants which say:
'You have the Right not to be Raped'.
But she is safe.
She has the Right to Education. But her paper school just blew away.
She has the Right to Medicine. But her paper pills give her stomach pains.
She has the Right to Freedom. But the paper key keeps bending in the prison lock.

She has the Right to Vote at the Polls. But her paper transport there ran out of paper gas
     and stopped.
But she is fine.
Lying 10 feet below buried safely under brand new copies of the
Universal Declaration of Human Rights.

A BRITISH NATIONAL BREAKFAST

They start the day with a small glass of orange juice.
Bought at Sainsbury's. South African produce.
Mugs emblazoned with our German-bred queen
they sip English breakfast tea,
forgetting it's Indian leaves.
1 and a half teaspoons each of sugar grain.
Asda bought. Barbadian cane.
Husband fries eggs. Wife waters wisteria.
Cooking oil from Italy. Heating oil, Nigeria.
They swallow two pills each
to help their bowels and digestion
invented by a research team of US and Indian.
Newspaper flicked through. Headlines are read:
Reads 'More Crime, More Violence, Less Hospital Beds'.
She complains to her husband, he complains to his wife.
They complain it must be those
'foreigners'
ruining their lives.
Voting polls open. BNP ticked
Pen bought from Staples. Iranian ink.
They drive home on roads laid by Irish Jamaicans.
She sprays on her perfume, an Arab invention.
Complaining about 'foreigners' joining their country,
forgetting the source of their dear British money.
Desperate for someone to blame for her boredom
she waters the pansies. Fertilizer from Jordan.
Desperate for someone to blame for his misery
they complain that 'foreigners' are ruining the country.
Afternoon nap to TV, both sigh.

Made in Sri Lanka. Sold from Shanghai.
Mumbling that Polish have run to their country
they watch *A Place in the Sun*
repeated from Sunday.
Shop down at Asda 'cause the stuff there is cheaper,
they complain:
'more British Jobs for more British people'.
Buy 2 for 1 offers from low wages abroad,
claiming:
'the price of local farm shops is robbery, fraud'.
Pick up a pizza on the short journey home,
complaining:
'British culture is being pushed to death row'.
Home on the couch. Watch TV all night.
Claiming that 'foreigners' have ruined their lives.
Finish their day with a cup of hot cocoa.
Beans made in Kenya. Profits to Tesco.
Complaining in bed about closing sea borders,
they don't learn Spanish. Retire to Majorca.

ALIVE

I wish I could soak up the sky in my eyes
feel the rain on my tongue when the cloud's running dry
taste the wind on my cheeks when the silence is high
I'm still waiting
still weeping with pride.
I wish I could trap every beam of light's heat
sleep in the sun when the shadow nights reap
breathe in snow breeze when the heat waves sweep
I'm still weeping, still dreaming so sweet.
I wish I could whisper the purple of sunsets
drip reds of the sunrise till my paintbrushes run wet
showers in plant scent and cut grasses sweat
I'm still dreaming, still feeling so blessed.
I wish I could lie on the tree tops of rainbows
float weightless on star paths while dark howls and wind blows
breathe out the planets like bubbles in earth glow
and lie back in sleepless black holes.
I wish I could witness each new bud give birth
feel every sandstorm and rain drip on dirt
I wish I could hear every petal unfurl
'cause I'm blessed to be alive in this world.

A STRIPPER'S UNIFORM

'We girls love a man in uniform.'
The Officer tops the charts
of stripper outfits set to thunder
females' horny hearts.
Richard Gere in brassy buttons
commanding sweaty men
in camouflage and two-step marches
'We love those manly men'.
Beyoncé sings a high-pitched shriek
she wants a 'soldier' in her life.
Trained and ready,
muscles pumped,
knife in mouth, machine-gun rife.
'We girls love a man in uniform',
a Captain, Sergeant, Sir.
But that officer and gentleman you see
for me there's nothing worse.
Sexy?
I don't see it
through Grandad's teary nightmares
of little boys, of friends of his
and dead, eyes rolled back stares.
Army chiefs of any fight
don't do it quite for me
sitting safe in board rooms
claims of helping history.
Strategy and high command
don't get me feeling wet

except perhaps in bitter tears
and angry, hateful, shaking sweats.
Parade that stripper uniform
like dismembered girls and boys,
separating army commander shouts
to why they're making noise.

All I see are women holding kids
dismembered limbs in bombs
as our officer sits sipping tea
cheering patriotic songs.
I hear the screams of waking women
from every living war
raped before their babies' eyes by bullies craving more.
Mothers' legs scraped apart with cries from husbands held
in torture dens with screams of men through fires burnt in fingernails.
I see soldiers marching on to fights in cultures they don't get,
no knowledge of the politics or why they're even sent,
I see scenes of furnaced cities, villages and towns,
hands scraping ash for loved ones burnt in rubble
bombing
drowned.
I see orphanages filled to brim, new refugees in flight,
future years of waking memories and cold sweats cried at night.
I see lifelong scars in brains or burns distorting faces shot,
single fathers coming home to dead loves and empty cots.
I see millions crouching, stomachs held, crying sobs of fear
and officers commanding troops that 'Victory' is near.
Calling bombs from fighter jets, obliterating homes
as strategy victorious and casualties unknown.
So though the Officer outfit tops the charts

the idea makes me sick
as if training guns on mothers' sons
is proof of bigger dicks.

So bring me a stripper anyday
dressed as Martin Luther King or Gandhi,
with muscly arms trained to massage
and bake.
Now *that* would make me randy.

BABY AND BOYFRIEND

When I watch them both sleep I want to bite both their cheeks.
I mean, his *and* hers.
I mean, face *and* bum.

BALLERINA

There are no more ballerinas
No more tap or jazz
No more dancehall teasers
No more breakdance gymnast fads
There's no more swing or salsa,
no more quick step, jive or twist,
just an MTV dance school teaching us to thrust and strip.
There's no more first position
just a vision of the Pussycats,
successful stripper dance troupe
got all the young girls doing that.
So instead of turns and smart moves we're just down to fuck the floor.
MTV dance lessons best at telling female dancers they're just whores.
From talent, pointed toes, healthy glows and spins from front to back,
it's lap dances, male stag parties with credit cards swiped down girls' cracks.
It was *talent*, baggy pants, t-shirts, leotards or bows,
now it's g-strings, wet t-shirt routines, front chair splits and bending low,
so ...
While MTV campaigns to make-believe a gorgeous, dancing, happy, healthy 'ho'
the dance teacher looks round crying:
'Where did all my female pupils go?'

BANANA BABY

I cupped my hands out in front of me, thinking
'your baby should be as big as a banana now'.
Email updates and pregnancy forums think my
'baby should be as big as a banana now'.
I cupped my hands in front of me, shaping them like the small fruit bowl I bought from the
craftswoman at the Saturday market who cried when I bought it and I thought she was
crying 'cause I was her only customer for the day, the week, the month maybe, battling with
Habitat factory-made fruit bowls but maybe she was actually thinking that day
'your baby should be as big as a banana by now'
'your sickness may calm down now'
'you should feel more tired now'
'you should put on a pound a week now
'you may be more forgetful now'
'your stomach may be sorer now'
'you should think about your finance now'
'you should consider birth classes now'
'you should book your next scan now'
'you should start pelvic exercises now'
'you should get the maternity leave form now and fill it in and hand it to your boss now'
'you should start thinking about names for the baby now'
'you should decide whether or not you are going to use disposable or cotton or semi-
disposable or eco-company nappies now'
'you should not sleep on your back or on your right-hand side now and sleep may be
uncomfortable now and you may wake in the night now and your ribs may ache now and
your left arm and shoulder and leg may hurt a little now and you may think about buying a
sculpted pregnant woman cushion now'
But don't do too much.
Remember to relax.
Maybe she was thinking that.
'Your baby should be as big as a banana by now'.

BOREDOM

L'ennui
c'est la mort
il tue l'amour
sa vue vous choque
il bloque les cœurs
est source de crimes
stealing dreams and blocking sun beams.
Boredom
more than death
a love bereft
laughs at your last breath
breeding crime
it lines your way.
Volant vos rêves, cachant soleil.

Boredom.
It stinks of shit.
From sewers seeps to streets to poison kids
preaching, it lies in gutters lined with broken kicks
deflated footballs, grime and teenage sick
in lines of coke and late-night shifts
it sniffs each day in painful habits
breeding like rabbits, vermin hatched
finding fun in grabbing handbags
like a hammock, sagging centres
minds left numb and stomachs emptied
it snatches fire-filled beating hearts
pouring water over sunken sparks
through stolen dreams and dawning lights

24

waits outside pubs for pointless fights
turns kids to hate and adults reeling
minds to crime and hands to stealing
with nothing left, nothing to do
turning towns to human zoos
caged and locked in pathways blocked
think of only cock or watching clocks
as young people wait and rot
labelled yobs by headline cops
nowhere to go, no breaths are baited
youth clubs closed and playgrounds gated
boredom reigns on teenage crowns
ghostly village, city, town
as others frown and walk away
looking down on youth today.
As children play now let us pray
boredom will not spoil their way.

BREASTS

No-one talks about it.
They whisper round it.
With tabooed torchlights.
We stumble down it.
I didn't read about it and I read a lot.
Like writer's block
they stop at breasts.
A naked chest and my breaths are sickened
They feed her.
You feel them,
and my nerve ends quicken
in panic
trying to manage the two in one body,
I've got two lives each night and you're both wanting on me.
From one room to the next I quick step through characters
dimlit rooms soothing like underwear lavender.
As we sit down at 6, she sips like Siddartha
my arms heat her belly and lips sleep in laughter.
Then after lights low, music sweet singing melodies
I step to the next room where he's waiting patiently.
From skin to skin baby
to skin to skin man,
from staring at innocence to staring at pants.
And it's hard,
it's so hard
to transfer position
in one step through one door in one dimlit partition
and I wish I could just split my body to two:
One chest held in sex

26

and the other to feed through.
And they make you feel sick and they make you feel strange
asking questions like 'when she's feeding is the sensation the same?'
When her tiny hands tap at the skin on your breast
of course it's not similar to strokes felt in sex
and we stress that it's strange or it's weird or it's wrong
when from lovely to lover our body moves on
when the space moves from pleasure to absolute pain
and your breasts move from caressing to milk-filled-up veins
and my brain took a long time to calm to the notion that souls shattered splinter and no-one
is wholesome.
In one body we each house infinite people.
From one door to the next split minds lock in feelings.
So I lay her to sleep and wipe off the milk
and step into the next room for some innocent filth
in the middle of which a scream jolts me up
and my breast moves once more between lover and love.

BUDDHA IN BROWN SLIPPERS

You were my Buddha in brown slippers.
Sitting on the sofa to meditate.
You had this face more peaceful than a baby's embrace.
You were my mountain,
you were my sky
and when the birds fly by now I can almost hear your sighs.
You were my clock ticks and tocks teaching me 'time will pass by'
but that's fine you said
that's just the timeline of life.
You were my guru, my love tunes and my pride,
you were everyone who ever met you's shining light
and when you told me I was beautiful inside
you were the stars' flicker flames I needed when I was burning at night,
you were the tear that trickled past my eye,
you were the fear I couldn't hide,
you were the tear I tried so hard not to let fall because you made me promise you I wouldn't
cry at your funeral at all.
But I couldn't keep that promise and
I'm sorry.
'cause you were my hoodlum,
my partner in crime,
taking out your false teeth to embarrass the family at dinnertime
you were my storyteller on the floor in my slippers
you were the cream soups you slooped crying 'bugger the doctors'.
You were my buddha in brown slippers,
my angel in pulled-up socks,
your halo handkerchief on your bald head in four knots,
you were the only grandad on the block who wore Nike,
you were my war stories you hated so much to tell me,

28

you were my restful reclining smiling spirit god
so when your heart beat stopped
and I know you said I better not
but I sobbed
and I'm sorry
sometimes I still can't stop.

BURNT BUTTERFLIES

So there's another red cross on the tree down her road, disease spreading so fast and none of them know why the seeds are all marked when they're perfectly healthy or why the men march past with chainsaws and machetes, 'cause this is their home, for generations gone by, now their grandma lies dead and their babies all cry so with her butterfly wings she flies high up to spy if the rest of the forest is this fucked. From the treetop canopy she sees the birds are all dead, can it be the whole bloody forest is emblazoned with red, man-made crosses of death on the breaths of the trunks, men chopping down chunks like they don't give a fuck that this is her throne, for centuries by she's been keeping a balance between the soil and the sky, now there's men marching by with matchsticks and poison, the shitty bit being, she was here way before them, in the forest and fauna beneath leafy umbrellas, now the forests grow smaller and the rains flood the rivers as the butterfly shivers with each thud, watching domino trees falling flat in the mud now she flutters between broken leaves and defeat, watching animal friends splutter half dead to their knees, matchsticks flicked on the floor now the forest's ablaze, and her wings stick together in the heat of the haze, 'cause this is shame, what we've done, shamed the earth, shamed the sun, if we could sell the moon, I'm sure we'd do it, if we could package the stars I'm sure we'd get a plan and get to it, but I'm sure something's coming, I'm sure those burnt butterflies are planning something, and when they come we better run, 'cause there's no excuse for the shit we've done to them.

No red cross on the tree, we burnt down the forests, started taking the seas and rape in raking the corals, now the fishes are swimming around in circles like madmen 'cause we tincanned all the dolphin and polluted the plankton, now there's no food in the seas, just raindrops dripping on leaves like oil puddles in oceans coating broken birds' beaks, pearl beads looking sweet on ladies' necks and shark teeth trophies adorning rich men's cupboards. On the floor of the ocean the last starfish waits for the black rope maze she spies coming her way, scraping the seabed of all flowers and rocks, as mumbled sounds resound from the humans laughing on the boat on top, her 5 legs frantically reversing on sand from the 6-mile net catching anything that stands, trapped dolphins and protected reefs, dead fish line the seas, the starfish stuck now she can't breathe. 'Cause it's a shame, what we've done, shamed the earth, shamed the sun, if we could sell the moon, I'm sure we'd do it, if we could package the stars I'm sure we'd get a plan and get to it. But I'm sure, something's coming, I'm sure those stuck starfish are planning something, and when they come we better run, 'cause there's no excuse for the shit we've done to them. 'Cause this is shame, what we've done, shamed our future daughters' and our sons' suns. We sold their forests for fifty quid, greedily drained their seas and turned their sun to darkness.

CHEMICAL KIDS

Our country's kids are covered in chemicals,
their lettuces are grown in test tubes,
the meals we feed them are making them hysterical
while the media blames sex, puberty and weed use.
As government campaigns pain me to choke
on Five Fruit and Veg a Day just another profit joke
with a punchline in the fields where those vegetables are grown
in cesspits of pesticides our babies' seeds are sown so no
that's not why mums go to Iceland
'cause a Ready Rustlers burger's not a life for any real pram
and even single working papas don't need ready frozen food
'cause pre-packaged plastic's never cheaper than a cookbook
so look
we're bringing up our babies on Heinz tin cans
when all we needed was a minute, masher, piece of fruit and saucepan.
So obsessed about the danger of bongs, condoms and kissing
when ingredients reek genocide of pesticides pissed in
food growing factories free of soil, air or insects
mother nature raped and staked by agriculture business
farmers forced to feed the land to fertilizer firms
as the need to feed our babies well becomes a need for greed to earn
pushing chemicals and pesticides and plastic packaged shopping
as profits rise for the guys who produce the chemicals we're popping,
so stop obsessing over your young boy trying out weed, wanking or wine
when you ignore the fact we can't even read the ingredients of his mealtime
and you can feed me all the lines you like but read the gravy label on the back, like
disodium ribonucleotides hydrolysed, modified acesulfame K sodium benzoate
tell me, what the fuck is that?
And you can read me all the laws you like till the cows might come back

32

but I'd rather smoke an illegal piece of leaf than eat your legal cyst-filled chicken wrap
wrapped round chickens trapped in lightless prisons pissing on each other
as deranged brain and bollock cocktail sausages bring up our future mothers
and father and sisters and brothers now covered in chemicals
with lettuces grown in test tubes
with carrots with no roots
with tomatoes sprayed with gas
mashed potatoes turned to smash
with bleach washed salad bags airtight with lies
and you can feed me all the adverts you like
but Cheese Strings will always be shite
and your Lunchables ham cheese lunchbox will never enter mine
and chickens bred in darkness will never bring light
and vegetables grown in chemically soaked test tubes will never be right
and you can feed me all the adverts and campaigns and prices you wish.
Just keep your food the fuck away from my kids.

DILEMMA

When she finally sleeps, I mean *finally* sleeps
like that eyes rolled back, lips apart deep kinda sleep
no peeks eyes relaxed, closed no leaks thick kinda sleep
heavy breaths keep to meeting heart beats kinda sleep.
When she finally sleeps, I mean *finally* sleeps
and our bed sheets haven't been seen for days kinda sleep
and it seems we've got three full hours before her next feed
and we sneak into bed and our legs want to weep,
finally, lying down, her father and me
the dilemma appears like a newborn brutality.
'Cause she finally sleeps, we can finally be
skin to skin, cuddled under the covers in glee
our giggling eyelids smile heavily
as we 'shoosh' at each sound that might wake the baby.
One kiss on your cheek to tell you goodnight
one kiss on your lips and a hand to your thighs
as your head wants to dream and there isn't much time
but the warmth of the back of your body on mine
three hours turns to two to tease me awake
and your breath feels so good on my aching neck nape
but each kiss that I give is one more minute awake
and I haven't slept well for at least seven days,
if I carry the play on, keep touching your face
we won't get the sleep our minds desperately crave,
fulfilling a space my skin endings ache
but I panic each second we're still both awake.
I wanna keep touching and I desperately don't
I want the hours to lengthen but they desperately won't
as I drift back and forth from your body to lone

34

and the bed drifts from sensual to sleep-giving throne
moaning, both body and mind
at the choice between sanity or feeling your sighs
the dilemma awakens each wonderful time
she finally sleeps
and your body's with mine.

D.I.L.F.

Since I've seen him change a nappy it seems his penis has grown,
muscles made more pronounced each time he folds those babygros.
His thighs were pretty buff before but since he's laid her on the floor,
one foot rocking her to sleep, the other touching toes with me
it seems his thighs are like three thousand times as juicy now.
Since I've seen him
push a pram
cook a meal with kid in hand
concoct a song to rock-a-bye
wake to cries with smiling eyes
pit stop challenge
changing kicks
cleaning rags of baby sick,
since I've seen him doing it
it seems his bits are twice as big, his lips are twice as ripe to kiss,
his neck nape twice as nice to lick.
I just have half the time to do it.
Since we've had a kid.

EACH NIGHT A DIFFERENT CAR PULLED UP OUTSIDE OUR FLAT

Each night a different car pulled up outside our flat.
In the heat of blackened Caribbean midnight hours our high-rise concrete cracks and three
electric cooling fans firing on our bodies couldn't stifle the sleepless naps
as we waited,
scared,
for him to come back.

Each night, a different car pulled up outside our flat of
two girls and one 'gay guy'.
We'd watch him from the balcony through our hazy smoke-filled eyes.
Stoned and scared.
Each night a different guy to share his heartache waited in our car park space.
We'd lay awake and wait till the dark ache of dawn
brought them back.

Each night a different car pulled up outside our flat.
He'd tell us that
he'd felt like that before, never quite that crap before.
He'd tell us that
he'd never had so much sex before but so little love.
So little connection but so much lust.
He said he'd never felt this way, so estranged from holding hands or making plans or feeling
it's ok to be a gay man.
He said he'd never had so much sex before but so little love
'cause fucks could be done behind the bare backs of wives on blackened beach sands or
round the back of the bricks of the blocks of our flats but love
that took more,
and love allowed,
that took laws.

37

He'd come back everyday from work in pain, tears streaking down his face.
He'd say in English class that day the teacher told the class to say
'Pédé'
translating paedophile in French to English gay, as if they were the exact same way,
and he'd stay quiet, tapping his foot through a new generation of mindwashed kids, biting
his lip like all the others like him did to keep his job.

Each night a different car pulled up outside our flat.
Faces scarfed by an island mentality where being gay didn't match being black.
Faces scarred by a land where being gay meant ok to attack.
And so they waited outside our flat
for him to go downstairs, the light-skinned European who might help to ease their fears.
He'd tell them tales of dates he had in Spain where two men walked and kissed in rain,
shared drinks in clubs, held hands, had time and space to love, heart and face ungloved.
Not like here,
where blackened alley gropes watched out for stares, where touch and lust led police and
cuffs and thugged up creeps where
dates were held on derelict beaches
broken backstreet cockroach huts
in undercover, uncomfortable, underground clubs
they asked him to tell them of love.

Each night a different car waited outside our flat.
Each night a different driver waited outside, flat.
Each night Daniel came back, flat.
Each night we chatted when he left the flat
spying through our concrete high-rise cracks
until they drove into the night
praying they'd both make it back
alive.

FRUIT AND VEG

In the UK, young girls cover their bodies with tanning paint,
to give pretend of foreign holidays or the illusion they're from a different race.
School girls spend days in pay-as-you-go tanning bays
in a quest for Spanish skin tones they're raising Scottish cancer rates.
But across the seas in India it's the opposite way
faces painted with skin creams for a paler, fairer taste
Brown to beige dreams seen in moisturising pastes
'Fair and Lovely' essence claims
your "destiny" will change
In Iraq, in Iran, in Afghanistan, female noses are being broken to resemble the token
      slimmer shape
whilst in Japan the fashion is slitting off girls' entire eyelids 'cause the US models have a
      more wide-eyed gaze.
In China the design is similar but the surgery takes no blood
instead of cutting off the eyelids they're simply flipped and stitched onto the skin above.
In South Korea, the face shape is the focus,
from the European beauty adverts, roundness must be changed to oval,
so in this wider-faced nation the facelift young girls seek
is to smash the jaw, take the bone out, to force a shape of slimmer cheeks.
In Ireland acid peels claim to dissolve freckles into dust,
in Uganda chemicals and wigs straighten curls and cover afros up.
Like the fruit and veg in Tesco's aisles, females blurring into one.
We've carrot colour charts and perfect sized tomatoes, straight teeth, solid boobs
      and uplifted bums.
So the next time you're in the supermarket for your weekly dash of plastic food
can you please demand they bring back wonky vegetables, organic girls and speckled
      multi-shaded fruit?

FUCKING ASYLUM SEEKERS

Fucking Asylum Seekers, he says, sitting on the sofa, hand on his crotch.
Fucking Asylum Seekers, he says, scratching and rearranging his bollocks.
Fucking Asylum Seekers, he says, flicking through shit daytime tv channels.
Fucking Asylum Seekers, he says, have you heard what they're up to now?
Fucking Asylum Seekers, he says, are seeking asylum in our damn country.
Fucking Asylum Seekers, he says, are sneaking our taxes, stealing our money.
Fucking Asylum Seekers, he says, they got it cushty coming to us.
Fucking Asylum Seekers, he says. Slamming the pages of the *Daily Mail* shut.

Fucking Asylum Seekers? I say
What the fuck were you?
Fucking Asylum Seekers? I say
In fucking World War Two?
Fucking Asylum Seekers? I say
Where the fuck would you have run, if the countryside you fled to was being bombed?

He opens the page again, looks at me, and points to the print with his self-engraved pen like
Yeah
Fucking Asylum Seekers, he reads, are taking our jobs, nah, living on social!
Fucking Asylum Seekers, I say, don't even get to get the dole.
Fucking Asylum Seekers, he reads, 25% of them on our soil!
Fucking Asylum Seekers, I say, its less than 2%, none at all.
Fucking Asylum Seekers, he reads, running to us for our free hospitals!
Fucking Asylum Seekers, I say, are running away to save getting killed.
Fucking Asylum Seekers, he reads, spouting the next page of fact-claiming fallacy.
Fucking *Daily Mail*, I say, educating our fucking families.

He turns his back on me.
Fucking Asylum Seekers, he says.

Reading, then believing, then speaking, then rearranging his bollocks.

He flicks to the next page.

Fucking paedophiles, he says, they're kidnapping kids everywhere!

Next page.

Fucking Muslims, he says, they're dropping bombs everywhere!

Next page.

Fucking gays, he says, they're spreading AIDS everywhere!

Next page.

Fucking Polish, he says, they're taking our jobs everywhere!

Fucking!

Next page.

Fucking!

Next page.

Fucking.

Fucking.

Fucking *Daily Mail*.

GRAVESTONE

I saved up all my life
For this.
And I love it.
When people see it they know that I'm rich.
Important.
Other people stare and admire it as I lay back.
Gold plated. Gold leaf engraved
R.I.P.
On my marble gravestone.
I couldn't afford any more words.

HOLLOW

We started quite similar, two young girls 'knocked up'
boyfriends excited and mums and dads chuffed
our friends buzzing by to put hands on our bumps
both belly and boobs getting shockingly stump.
We started quite similar, both bellies slow rising
two plum ripe tomatoes grow stretch marks in lines.
While we're both walking home after work in the office
we try not to waddle as passers-by's eyes are on us.
We started quite similar, both woken at dawn
to two kicks in the pelvis, both giggle and yawn.
Now she lies at the side of the road simply screaming
I'm home, she just groans, both our feet up, hers bleeding.
'Cause there's no march going on in my city you see
no war so that war crime's not used against me
I might walk the streets hunchback but baby lies safely
and whilst mine may be chocolate, it's revenge that she's craving.
So when you ask what I'm thinking, is it boots, cots or mittens
truth is, I'm just thankful it's here that I'm living,
'cause as my stomach bulges like a water balloon
her hollowed-out body lies like carcass consumed
in the wrong time, the wrong street, the wrong country or place
on the wrong side or the wrong tribe, the wrong party or race.
Both trying not to waddle as passers-by's eyes all watched,
but whilst mine passed me by, hers circle and stop.
Radio announcements as troops told to target
mothers, children, unborn moses baskets
with knives and machetes like cutting through ham
they slice round her belly to remove what they can.
We started quite similar, two young girls knocked up,

43

my boyfriend excited, hers hung himself up.
My mum and dad chuffed, her mum and dad mourning
and as flies buzz her belly, my friends' hands still swarming.
'Cause there's no war going on in my city you see
no radio orders to ethnically cleanse me.
So when you ask what I'm thinking with a baby inside me
my hands clasp the skin tight and my mind runs in hiding.
So when you ask what I'm thinking, is it cots, toys or clothes,
I just smile and nod 'cause truth is I don't know.
So when you ask what I'm thinking everytime that it kicks
ask what I think when its heart beats so quick
the thing I think most, though it might sound quite sick
is how on earth could you cope if they cut out your kid?
But there's no war going on in my city you see
so that war crime's not used as a weapon against me
no knife waiting bluntly to cut through my womb
as her body lies clutching a hollowed-out tomb.
The thing I think most, and it's making me sick
is how on earth could you cope if they cut out that kid?

LANGUAGE LEARNING

You make my toes curl up in two languages, my heart pump across the Channel, and as the
beat gets faster, the waves race after my thoughts flicking from London to Paris. 'Cause when
I think of you in English my lips begin quivering a little bit, I begin giggling like a little kid
and when you ask me to go for a drink at the pub after 7 years I still feel a little sick. I panic.
Matchstick legs that might buckle and break as butterflies take flight fluttering up in my belly,
my breaths get heavy every time you put your hand in my hand,
smile at me and kiss my cheek gently I turn to jelly and ice cream.
But see
when I think of you in French it's somehow different.
My nervousness switches off as you transform from
'mon copain' to 'mon amant'.
You're not funny or sweet in French,
it's like this heat-fuelled meat-treat physical thing in French, non,
je ne pense plus à toi comme drôle ou mignon, non.
In French, je pense à tes hanches, your hips, tes jambes, your lips,
ton grand, your big, grand, big,
coeur.
Je pense de tes cuisses, tes boutons de soleil et je veux me bronzer sur la plage de ton body
        all day,
I just wanna pull up my deckchair on your chest there and laze.
Sans jamais arrêter.
In French, it's like intense passion.
I imagine feeding you croissants sur la plage just splashing, sipping a little wine, slipping
        a little time just to stare into tes yeux brown eyes.
In English, I get embarassed and prudish getting nude or talking dirty
but in French it's so damn easy for me de 'fantasiser':
Je peux dire ce que je veux, à toi
et parce que tu ne comprends pas je peux dire les choses que je ne dirais point en anglais.
In French, I might ask if I could lay you down pour te deshabiller, te sucer.

But in English I would never say strip or suck!
In French, I might ask if we could baiser.
But in English I'm too shy to even utter the word F.U.C.K.
So you see,
you make my toes curl up in two languages,
it's like I've got two men, two best friends,
I've got this horny Paris lover hidden under my loving Luton boyfriend's bed
I've got two men, deux hommes, deux sentiments, deux bites alors,
two tongues, two kicks, two types of bliss.
Best bit is, right now, I'm learning Spanish.

MERMAIDS

I hope they find you baby
on play-mat ocean floors
I hope they make you seaweed sheets and wrap you warm on sandy reefs
I hope the corals sway for you your oyster rattles clutched in hands,
pearls shake with open-eyed amazement watching seahorse bubble bands.
I hope the mermaids sing for you and curve the waves to lull your sleep
I hope your tears are wiped by mother octopuses' eight great feet
I hope you land so softly babies, float onto the ocean's floor

and hope that we learn up above to welcome people to our shores

to help them out of fleeing boats and let them live upon our lands
too late for you I pray you both sank safely into mermaids' hands.

MR IMPORTANT

He thinks he's so very important, driving around in his red Porsche with his portable Walkman, looking down as he walks past the porters and doormen forced to open doors for him as if he's someone they ought to respect, as if he's doing such good staying in fourstar hotels, sipping bordeaux and cordon bleu, fancy food chewing buttoned up designer suit and he's made it. In the mirror he winks to himself at his greatness. Now he thinks he's so very important, shoes are polished, gleaming bright like the trophies adorning his mantelpiece, blocking his children's drawings and family photos, only his business awards cover the walls of his boat-home. He thinks he's so very great. City banker with a bonus higher than the average salary wage, waiting for pay day to buy another villa in Spain, waiting for a minute to check his guerilla shares have risen again. He thinks he's so very important, world revolves around him like he's the magnet in orbit, North-South poles from his head to his toes, making decisions with hand shakes, breaking targets and goals. He thinks he's so very great, better than the other men and women cleaning his floor and washing his plates, making jokes to his mates about the cleaners he pays like slaves, making jokes to his mates about his drivers and how he bends over his maids. He thinks he's so very important 'cause he's got a 9-inch TV screen on the wall of his toilet so he can watch with enjoyment while he's taking a shit, looks down before he flushes as if expecting specks of gold dust in it.
He thinks he's so very great.
Unfortunately.

At his funeral.

No-one came.

MS NATURE

There's a fantasy outside, but no-one knows about it,
boxed up in flats, offices and houses without it,
step outside, can't believe what you're missing,
wander into fields and feel mother nature kissing
clouds overhead, like a jungle, stumble in a clearing
with two buds on your tongue, chase the light, now you're shrinking
through the hole,
lights out like childhood power cuts fumbling
through fallen leaves, weed and flowers,
hear the rabbits shout,
people come our way,
get off your roads, release your mind for this high play,
the gloomy city's long gone,
Ms Nature's gonna kiss you,
look around you for a minute,
let sweet trees tickle you.

Come play away, lay away your days in my haze man.
Come stray away let my crazy forest glade man.
Pick up a branch, spark a plant and light your way man
breathe in and listen to the sounds of the forest like:

Sweet sweet, sipping on buttercup tea,
tweet tweet, hear the nightingales' and butterflies' glee
beat beat, the forest drums under basted trees
sit back and listen to Ms Nature's melody.

Life here, she slowly whispers in your ear,
it's so nice here, there's nothing here for you to fear.

49

All that you like here, my mother surely provides,
you're living a nightmare back home
with your nine-to-fives.

And I start thinking, watching the grasshoppers parade,
What was I thinking?
As I lie on flowers under leafy shade
I'm sinking into petals, sweet perfume washes a fragrant phase of fireflies,
lighting the glade like a star parade.
It's so beautiful here, I'm not going back.
It's so musical hear
crickets, bluebells and blades of grass
breezing in the sunshine's path,
basking me in wild mushrooms, gooey honey
and real love at last.
I take a walk,
see a fairy ride a lizard
snakes whisper breezes
and butterflies kissing.
Listen.
Frogs playing with pixies
hopping onto lily pads
and splashing the fishes,
I'm wishing,
I could stay here forever
naked like the others
living life a little better
eating chestnuts and acorns
bathing in oceans' ponds
living to live
just living with nature's song

so Ms Nature
please keep
caressing me.
I'm floating along so
please keep addressing me.
I'm rolling
along up upon the back of this centipede
just keep singing your song,
bless me.

There's a fantasy outside, but no one knows about it,
boxed up in flats, offices and houses without it,
step outside, you won't believe what you're missing,
wander into fields and feel mother nature kissing
clouds. But people stare at the pavement.
There's beauty all around us but the beauty's been wasted,
we tasted the way
so go now and share it
there's a playground around you,
make others aware of it
stare at it
smell it, touch it and taste it,
look up to the sky because people just waste it,
look up to the sky because people never do,
steel trees, oil rivers, concrete jungle swamping you.
Look around you
at the people filled with beauty
'cause we've trained our tired eyes to recognise
nothing but Gucci.
Look intensely at material
and miss everything godly, it's cold.

We didn't make the bodies to distract you
from the soul.
It's cold.
We didn't make the money to distract you
from the real gold.
There's a world outside, but people too scared to go there,
woods aren't full of frights, don't believe all you're told, there
aren't terrorists and thieves lurking in the trees,
just fantasies and freedom floating
in between the leaves.

MY BOYFRIEND CAN COOK

I'm sitting slightly tipsy sipping from a bottle of white wine
taking my time
watching my man like a fine dine.
Aphrodite the mighty god
blessed me.
He's cooking for *me*.
It's wet and messy.
He's peeling the sautéed potatoes, I'm tasting
spicy aromas
smelling like cravings
bathing naked
in the scent from the cooker.
I look at him.
He smells sweet like a pod of vanilla.
Rosemary buds, hot pepper, thyme and steam
a little sweat drips from his brow and it's time to dream
I imagine lying naked in a field of strawberries
drowning in custard and cream, I'm getting sore, please.
He wipes his face. A little glance my way
sipping on his liquor, my lips ready to play.
Stray sizzling colours mix with sensual smells
my body sweat mingles waiting for that tingle from the timer's bell.
I want to yell, but I sit there caressed,
eyeing up
steaming pans on hobs like clouds of sweet breath.
He's just making dinner, I'm making babies in my head.
He passes me asparagus tips soft dressed in lemon
tickling my tongue as I suck them
then I'm licking on the starter melon.

Sweet juice from the fruit running down my chin
a little giggle, juice trickles down my nipples and g-string.
The potatoes are boiling,
oil heating like a piece of warm skin
I imagine my body so oily boiling on top of him.
It's nearly time.
As red wine like deep sighs he pours into the sauce
I'm getting wet just waiting for his main course.
Hard wooden spoon he holds stirring that gravy
circular motion, soft, firm, like when he makes me come.
Adds some rum,
a pinch of pepper and salt
candles flicker, knickers wet
as he takes the pot.
Now I'm standing by the cooker in a loose dress
his hand dips in the sauce and I taste it off his
slow motion, my warm lips wrapped round his finger
slow pulling and as the fresh flavours linger
in my mouth
my tongue tastes the rest of
broccoli and green beans
cream sauce and sweetness
dripping taste from my thighs to my chest.
My plate is licked clean.
My tastebuds hurt.
I lie back, already ready
for dessert.

ON ACID

I'm living a life of half dreams
sleep interrupted in breast milk streams
adventures broken in 2am screams
eyes open and closing like counting machines
between 2 hour shifts where I swap with me.

I'm living a life of half dreams
cellophane flowers and tangerine trees
rowing down milk rivers through breast hill valleys
to nipple cream islands in cold cups of tea.

I'm living a life of half dreams
comotosed arms rock automatically
tiny lips to my breast my mind tries to see
if she's just fed and I've fallen or if she's waiting to feed
if she's just fed or she's hungry or if I'm already asleep.

I'm living a life of half dreams
asleep with ears open checking she breathes
staring at ceilings to birds' melodies
singing in day as I drift back to sleep.

I'm living a life of half dreams
stories stolen by waking bellies
body jolts upright with every night scream
eye bags, arm muscles, and breasts are heavy,
I'm ready in every half dream
waking to two big eyes staring at me

with a fist stuffed in mouth to ease the need
as she waits for my waking with impatient greed.

I was lying in bed. Wake up. Breastfeed.
I was dreaming I slept. Wake up. Breastfeed.
I was dreaming we kissed. Wake up. Breastfeed.
I was dreaming your lips. Wake up. Breastfeed.
I was sleeping. She wept. Wake up. Breastfeed.
I was awake as she slept. Wake up. Breastfeed.
I fell asleep as she fed. Wake up. Breastfeed.
I woke up as you said, 'Wake up. Breastfeed.'
She finished. She smiled. Our eyes met.
Wake up. Breastfeed. It's blessed.

PHOTOSHOP

I never spent too much time looking
just got on with being me
until you came my way and showed me all the possibility.
Now I realise I need focus and the space is there to dream
a life of perfect vision if you would just Photoshop me please,
'cause I think I'd be more eased with a hint of rose on blue
my eyes to match my ideal mag,
first change of one or two.
If you could Photoshop my chest too
my breasts a little bigger
my upper lip a little thicker
my hips into viola curves and my waist two inches trimmer.
And while you're there
could you Photoshop my freckles into peach-toned perfection
brush my Scottish skin with tanning paints and a light brown correction
stretch my legs a little longer, stop the hairs from growing on them.
Just Photoshop me please.
And while you're there
could you Photoshop my personality?
Make me funny, smart and sassy
flip depressed to ever happy.
And while you're there
could you Photoshop my family?
Photoshop my angry tears, merge my homelands back together,
smashed flat windows and heart breaks whole forever,
better Photoshop the black eye from my mum's dear friend, ooh and Photoshop that bullet
hole embedded in her chest as well, edit her and her son's name from the engraved
gravestone head and maybe Photoshop her husband's hand from the triggered piece of lead.
And while you're there

could you Photoshop that dole queue, those soup kitchens and the shelters
replace those street kids with blonde scouts and those bins with helter skelters?
Photoshop the refugee camps, UN guards and barbed wire heights
cut and paste a more tasteful desert frame, singalongs and campfire nights.
And when it's dark
could you Photoshop the homeless into warm bubbled glows,
brush the flies from those kids' faces into neon coloured rainbows?
Could you
Photoshop the who-knows, the who-cares and the give-a-damn?
Photoshop the sex trade into girls paid to take exams?
Photoshop extinctions back to fields and seas,
indigenous people back onto the lands they live and breathe?
Could you
Photoshop the weapons deals, the money sharks and fat cats?
Photoshop the greed, cut want for need and paste that?
Photoshop the world flat, ours eyes blind and mouths shut?
Photoshop our minds numb, brains dumb and hands up?
Surrendered to our mirrors, possessed by self reflections
motionless mannequins in Photoshop obsessions.

PULL UP

As I sit listening again I'm just sickened again of this
same story
the same beat
the same breaths slowing underneath
the rubbles,
again.

The headline read: 'Morro dos Prazeres: Las autoridades sabian del riesgo'.

'Morro dos Prazeres'.
Just the latest track to hear
on a record scratching back to black every bloody year.
Drowned in 'pull ups' as Selecta hands
rewind the news words back,
pulling up from ash and ice melts
new bodies flattened slack.
Same global track, same worldwide flow
as news reports claim help was slow
and victims shout what we all know: 'Las autoridades sabian del riesgo!'
The authorities knew the risk.
And did shit. Before disaster hit.

'Cause those who live in a place like this are just not that important
to those who live in palaces and politicians' quarters
so where they ought to build, they don't,
no barriers, no safer roads,
no leakless roofs, no thicker stone,
just stick and straw and paper homes
'cause those who live in a place like this are just not that important

to GDP or policy or economic borders
and so the track winds back again.
And loved ones mine through ash again.
Landslides slide through shacks again.
Favelas collapse in grime again.
Hurricanes stop time again.
Melting ice moves tribes again.
Forests burnt cuts lives again.
And no-one helps till time again
it's just too bloody late
and the record skips to play
the same old bassless flow: 'Las autoridades sabian del riesgo'.
The authorities knew the risk.
And waited till disaster hit
a place like this. Again.

SOUP KITCHENS

It's not that you're rich, it's that you're really fucking rich
like three holidays a year is not that dear, really rich
like you have that ruddy winter tan from sun-soaked Bahamas trips
in December, just 'you know, to get a bit of heat' really rich.
It's that your student loan was put into an isa really rich.
And uni fees were less than your school fees really rich.
And you've never waited tables or been a till assistant rich
because at weekends you drove to see the Hiltons really rich

So when you say that the change of soup kitchen laws is necessary, that giving a free bowl of
soup should be banned because it encourages people to choose a homeless life of freezing
cold streets, the humiliation of begging for food, money or help and the constant danger of
sleeping rough I just can't help thinking I've had enough. I can't even be arsed to rhyme if
these are the people leading the country.

Fuck.

TOOTHPASTE

I see the best minds of my generation starving hysterical naked,
scientific masters stripped bare in L'Oréal labs inventing more haircare age-defying night creams never drying lipsticks and baldness remedies.
I see puddles of pure engineering genius wringing out the blankets they could've weaved, a thousand solar panels stitched through Saharan farms like patchwork fields sat back in offices designing designer wheels for designer prams for designer mums in Shoreditch.
I see chemists covering lies in long white coats minds broken from years of lost equations salivating over all-in-one toothpaste, mouthwash, breath fresheners and complicated three-striped colour systems. Future formulae for disease eradication forever dried up in the necessity for dazzling smiles and minty freshness and an easy life.
I see architecture's visionaries grinding down lost pencils across more Dubai hotel complexes, jacuzzi-laden plans scribbled over the masterplans of water wells and makeshift drains and slum-saving sewage systems they were going to sketch yesterday.
I see sexless physicists on Sony payrolls controlling soundwaves for new studios and iPod speaker phone systems as earthquake tremors and cyclones and tsunamis go undetected.
I see science rejected, brains hanging out of heads like dead dreams as a million masterpieces remain unconceived under new hair creams and designer prams and baldness remedies.

WHEN THE SUN SETS

I want to go somewhere where the day ends when the sun sets
where neon lights and nightclub strips haven't been invented yet
where streets lights are fireflies
and eyes become accustomed to moon rays
and we awaken when the sunlight of day breaks.

I want to go somewhere where the day ends when the sun sets
and discotheques are beach beds of stamping feet and heads
and DJs are instruments and drum 'til toes are bled
and washed in dusk-dark oceans
and we awaken with the waves lapping gently over tired legs.

I want to go somewhere where the day ends when the sun sets
and rain is praised with wet hands
thanking skies for fresh lips smacked
and smiles passed like salt and pepper before we lie to rest
and we awaken with sunlit eyes and clear heads.

I want to go somewhere where the day ends when the sun sets
and dark skies mean stay in bed
instead of hedgehogs spying us through leafy piles
as mad men run through night-time skies to morning work
and we awaken in the afternoon after the sun's return.

I want to go somewhere where the day starts when the moon sets
and legs follow the sunrise into conscious breaths and muscles stretched
where dreams are only interrupted with a turned earth met
with the sun light and warm skies once again.
And we go to sleep when the sun sets.

WILLIES ARE MORE DANGEROUS THAN GUNS

I learnt this from censorship, the government, films and television.
Willies are much more dangerous than guns.
Especially when the owner of that willy has a hard'un.
So I just don't understand what I must've missed or if there's something about a man's bits I
haven't quite understood.
'Cause we ban penises on TV as if they're some magic concoction to turn teenagers into
sex addicts and kill all children who watch them, as if the sight of this six-inch slug
between a man's thighs could burn down family ties and destroy peoples' lives.
I know men call it their magic wand but it's really not that powerful,
a little tool to wave around it's really not that bountiful
and they might call it their cannon, but it's really not that large
and the cannon balls it sometimes shoots out really aren't that hard
and as soldiers go, as I've heard it called, it's just a little weak
'cause even when it's stood to attention it's normally ready to sleep.
But still.
Willies are more dangerous than guns.
Even when shooting blanks they are our enemy number one, so I just don't understand what
I must be missing or if there's something about a man's bits I haven't quite got a grip on yet.
'Cause as we pollute, loot and shoot British bullets into blazing nights
we teach our children that this piece of skin is a more frightening sight than dropping bombs
on children in Iraq like sick falling sweets, selling weapons worldwide waging war on the weak.
While we burn down more forest to produce more fake needs,
spill oil into seas, spread disease and kill species
TVs and we teach our children that Rambo and Van Damme are cool
but a boy with an erection is a 'sick and dirty fool',
that that man on the hot bus with an uncontrollable, embarrassing lift is not a biological
twitch but a 'sick old pervie git'.
We pay for plastic guns and water pistols to entertain our kids
but under absolutely no circumstance let them see a dick.

64

We stare at bloody bodies bullets broken bones and starving kids
but banned from seeing naked bodies: male or female 'special' bits.
I know I must be missing something 'cause otherwise it seems a little silly
to teach people they can play with guns but not with their own willies.
The government's most censored image. Our public enemy number one.
Please, tell me what I'm missing
if willies
are more dangerous
than guns.

WOW

WOW
My body is amazing!
I can almost hear her saying it
as she stands naked at the mirror
hands clapping in applause to it.
Naked, bold and proud
her mouth open wide and round like
Wow!
My body is amazing.
She's one year old and loving it
full belly sticking out, thighs like mini tyre towers
and when she looks at her reflection she always shouts aloud like
Wow.
This body is so great.
Gazing down now
I try to do the same.
Ignore the plastic advert spreads
that pass me on the way
I say 'my body is amazing'
despite what some might say
I say 'my body is amazing'
despite the claims you make.
The nip and tuck and cuts and sucks that fill my walk to work each day
enhancement ads and happiness will only come with curves this way and
if I lay in front of you today
clothes dropped to the floor
you'd prescribe me what I could have less of and what I should want more of.
A tick box what could be chopped off with red pen ready hand aside your eyes deciding what
to slice from lips and cheeks to bum to thighs.

The lines below my eyes you say
I ought to peel or pull away
my breasts will start to sag one day
my breastfed baby there to blame.
She came into the world, you say
that's great
but now behold your face
your saggy stomach, baggy eyes
stretch mark stripes you look and sigh:
My eyes, tighten.
My legs, inject.
My thighs, cut back.
My head, perfect.
My stomach, flatten.
My breasts, enhance.
Don't smile, too much,
oh God, don't laugh.
As you mark me like a canvas page in circled bouts of red
I feel the need to tell you you might praise this skin instead
'cause as you chat about corrections, your plucking cuts and lasers
briefcase stuffed with time relapses, scalpel-led erasers
I take up your red pen to my cheeks and mark two stripes on either side,
a naked painted warrior could be a sorer site for eyes 'cause
I am ready for your battles now
my body's felt the worst
no scalpel cut intense as that last damn push of birth
and I have learnt with awed amazement what my body brave can do
and now I'm marked like tribal tattoos with the tales my flesh went through.
But those stripes that line my saggy stomach mark me like gold
and the folds below my eyes tell a tale just as bold.
My laughter lines are deeper now because I smile twice as much

so if you palm-read these first 'wrinkles' my life would light up.
Your official position is that smoothness is queen
but without any lines there's no reading between them.
A storybook opening
my life's just begun and
once upon never plays
if I cling to line one
as you try to cover the living I've done
as a human, a woman, and now as a mum.
But your red pen can't rub out the nights I've not slept, the parts that I've bled or the
laughter I've wept, the baby I held in my stomach that stretched, the breasts that got heavy so
baby was fed, the parties I've had out, the sleep I've missed out on, the dinners I've stuffed
down my throat like a python,
as you pile on the pressure to cover my life
I wonder what the hell is so wrong with your sight.
If my mind and my memory can tell you my tales
then why can my body not tell them as well?
As our babies lie naked,
applauding their skin
I can't wait for their lives *and* their lines to begin.

NOTES ON THE POEMS

These are all triggers for the poems. They are part of bigger influences but are the specific things I remember when I think of them.

A BRITISH NATIONAL BREAKFAST (p 15)

A customer in the clothes shop where I worked would stand and complain about every immigrant group in Britain, at the end of which he revealed he had moved to Spain because of it. 'Do you speak Spanish?' I said. Course not, no need. The book *Immigrants: Your Country Needs Them* by Philippe Legrain, was one of many references I looked through in response.

A STRIPPER'S UNIFORM (p 18)

My papa (grandfather) used to tell me not to believe anything about the good of war. I wrote this after reading the novel *Guernica* by Dave Boling and drifting in and out of the novel, mixed with memories about my granddad's war stories and visions of a stripper my friends and I hired when we were 17. He dressed as Richard Gere from *An Officer and a Gentleman*. It was the number one choice on the list. It was an awful night. My papa also used to strip as a joke – he was better!

BANANA BABY (p 23)

Babycentre email updates came weekly when I was pregnant and they always compared the size of the fetus to fruit and vegetables. The mental pressures of pregnancy can be as heavy as the belly.

BOREDOM (p 24)

Another No Ball Games sign put up by the local council in another rare green space in a nearby housing estate. Boo. Thanks to Cindya Izarelli, Neil Elliot and Deejay Fira for French tips.

BUDDHA IN BROWN SLIPPERS (p 28)

For Papa with all my love x

BURNT BUTTERFLIES (p 30)

Inspired by a beat by UK hip hop group Taskforce. Recorded to the beat on *Touch*: audio album.

D.I.L.F. (p 36)

I think men are left out of the whole M.I.L.F. scene! Dedicated to a great dad and partner. (If you don't know the word M.I.L.F., watch *American Pie*.)

EACH NIGHT A DIFFERENT CAR PULLED UP OUTSIDE OUR FLAT (p 37)

After a year living in Guadeloupe, French West Indies, with a lovely flatmate; his tales and tragedies. A very strange experience living within a gay scene on an island where no-one admitted anyone on the island could be gay.

FRUIT AND VEG (p 39)
Written amidst claims that Scotland's skin cancer rate was overtaking sunny Australia's, due to tanning salons. Glasgow had trials to teach girls in school how to apply fake tan to curb sun bed use. I walked through George Square where a huge advert for H&M covered the public space in bikini clad olive-skinned models amidst pale, freckled Scottish crowds. Then I saw a Unilever product 'Fair and Lovely', a skin product which had as its motto 'Fairness that changes your destiny'. This was on the website: http://www.unilever.com.lk/brands/personalcarebrands/FairandLovely.aspx

FUCKING ASYLUM SEEKERS (p 40)
The *Daily Mail* Effect was a concept talked about by my professors when studying forced migration / immigration. Since then, every copy of the paper I see has something negative about immigrants / immigration, asylum seekers and refugees.

GRAVESTONE (p 42)
Bling inspired. MTV hip hop video inspired. Ghetto 'Fabulous' inspired. Friends who have no money left but lots to 'show' inspired.

HOLLOW (p 43)
I read *Half the Sky* by Nicholas Kristof and Sheryl Wudunn while I was pregnant. My mum bought it for me. I could no longer complain about my pregnancy after reading the women's stories in this book. There is a lot to be done.

LANGUAGE LEARNING (p 45)
For Gee x

MERMAIDS (p 47)
Written after articles in March 2011 about the 61 people who died on their boat just off the coast of Tripoli, Libya, including two babies. March 2011 *Guardian* headline which provoked the poem: AIRCRAFT CARRIER LEFT US TO DIE, SAY MIGRANTS.

MS NATURE (p 49)
Cycling through a local country park after 2 days in Central London listening to a beat by Toe. This came into my head. Recorded to the beat on *Touch*: audio album.

MY BOYFRIEND CAN COOK (p 53)
Watching my boyfriend cook veggie spaghetti bolognese whilst reading Isabel Allende's recipe book/novel entitled *Aphrodite*. Amazing book.

PULL UP (p 59)
2010 news coverage of the landslide which
wiped through Brazilian favela town Morro
dos Prazeres. Repeated phrase over internet
coverage, 'Las autoridades sabian del riesgo':
the authorities knew the risk.

SOUP KITCHENS (p 61)
Within all the fuss about the UK
conservative John Patten attempting to rid
his Westminster Borough of Soup Kitchens
or handouts to homeless people, under
claims it encourages sleeping rough.

TOOTHPASTE (p 62)
The profit motive in medical research
leading to research and funding aimed more
at issues like impotence and baldness than
the various tropical diseases that affect
millions.

WOW! (p 66)
The most frequent question I have been
asked since motherhood – are the stretch
marks really bad? What oil do I use? Makes
me sad and bored of this focus of every
aspect of a female's life, even after labour and
no sleep for a year. We should be bloody
proud.